Original title:
Bark Bits and Brambles

Copyright © 2025 Creative Arts Management OÜ
All rights reserved.

Author: Gabriel Kingsley
ISBN HARDBACK: 978-1-80567-268-5
ISBN PAPERBACK: 978-1-80567-567-9

Murmurs in the Nocturnal Thicket

In the dark where shadows creep,
Animals chatter, secrets to keep.
A raccoon wears a tiny cap,
While owls debate in a wise old nap.

A fox jumps out, a dance so bold,
Tripping over roots like stories told.
The moon giggles in its silver light,
As frogs croak tunes of sheer delight.

Sanctuary of the Untamed Wilds

Beneath the trees where squirrels leap,
A sleepy bear's in dreamland deep.
A rabbit hops with a comical flair,
Dodging twigs without a care.

A deer prances, looking quite grand,
While mice have formed a rock band.
The songs of crickets fill the air,
As laughter floats without a care.

The Art of Nature's Contrasts

Colors clash in a vibrant show,
A butterfly's chaos in dazzling flow.
Grass tickles toes, so lush and green,
While muddy puddles play hide and seek.

A sunflower bows to the light of day,
As bees zoom by in a wobbly way.
The artistry of nature is quite absurd,
Making even a plant feel like a bird.

Treading Softly on the Roughened Earth

With every step, a tiny crunch,
Acorns scatter in a playful bunch.
Stumbling over roots as I walk,
The trees around me seem to talk.

A chipmunk squeaks, "Watch where you tread!"
As leaves rustle secrets; I can't bear the dread.
Each footprint's laughter echoes wide,
In this wild world, I take my stride.

Whispers of the Woodland Night

In the moonlight, owls take flight,
Squirrels plot their midnight bite.
The raccoons dance with wild delight,
While badgers snore, what a sight!

Frogs croak jokes, all in tune,
While fireflies twinkle like silly balloons.
The trees whisper secrets to the moon,
And the night giggles, a joyful boon!

Twisted Roots and Silent Shadows

A tree trunk found a funky hat,
The roots complained, 'We're getting flat!'
But then they laughed, 'Oh, imagine that!'
The squirrels played ball with a friendly cat!

The shadows wiggled in moon's soft light,
While a raccoon put on a puppet show tonight.
The woodland critters laughed till they laid,
In the tangled vines, dreams were made!

Thorns in the Thicket

Prickly things can cause a fuss,
But bunnies bounce without a fuss.
The hedgehogs giggle, quite a plus,
As they roll right by, all in a rush!

A fox with flair, looks quite absurd,
Dressed up in twigs, but looks a bit blurred.
He winks and prances, so assured,
In thickets filled with laughter, unheard!

Secrets of the Forest Floor

Beneath the leaves, a party brews,
With mushrooms dancing in their shoes.
The ants march in, all with their views,
While a spider weaves tales of secret cues.

The saplings sway to a breezy beat,
While beetles tap dance, quick on their feet.
This hidden realm, with laughter sweet,
Holds secrets that no one can defeat!

Queries of the Woodland Breath

In the woods, a squirrel pranced,
Hiding nuts, while birds just danced.
"Why's your stash so full of treats?"
He winked and said, "I love my eats!"

Frogs in suits held a night debate,
Arguing if flies are fate.
"My dear friend, you'd make a feast,
But I prefer my flies with yeast!"

A raccoon donned a shiny crown,
Declared himself the king of town.
"Pay your taxes, fuzzy few!"
All laughed, then quickly bid adieu.

In the dark, the owls would hoot,
"Who ate all the woodland loot?"
They hooted loud, it caused a scene,
Turns out it's just a silly dream!

Chronicles of the Verdant Wilds

In the thicket, hedgehogs hold,
Secret meetings, tales retold.
"Who stole my blanket?" one did wail,
"It's just a leaf, don't send a mail!"

Badgers in a fancy dress,
Went a'waltzing, made a mess.
"Let's invade the farmer's yard!"
"But they've got gates, and fences hard!"

Bumblebees with tiny hats,
Buzzing close to dancing cats.
"Join our party, get in line!"
But cats just yawned, and won't decline.

The trees conspire with the breeze,
Whispering songs with growing ease.
"Will it rain, or shine today?"
"Let's just play and float away!"

A chipmunk thinks he's quite the chef,
Cooking acorns, but what a mess!
"Tasty snacks for every guest!"
Turns out, no one likes that fest!

Sprigs of Solitude and Serenity

In a garden where odd things grow,
A snail had a hat, and a frog wore a bow.
Squirrels played chess in the soft morning light,
While ants formed a band, what a wonderful sight!

One cactus recited a poem of woe,
While shadows danced lightly, with a glimmering glow.
The daisies all giggled at the bees in a swirl,
And the wind whispered secrets, oh what a world!

Tapestries Stitched with Nature's Thread

A bear wore a vest made of leaves and of fluff,
He boogied with hedgehogs, who challenged his stuff.
The winds hummed a tune that was catchy and sweet,
As rabbits in shoes tapped their little rabbit feet.

A fox in a top hat gave a welcoming grin,
A party of mushrooms began to break in.
The sun brought them cake, as it dripped from the sky,
While ants served the punch, waving gently goodbye!

Whispers of Time in Twisting Vines

Old tree branches joked as they swayed to the breeze,
With squirrels on stilts juggling acorns with ease.
A badger in spectacles read from a book,
While worms held a concert in a cranny or nook.

Yet up in the branches, a frog told a tale,
Of pies made with crickets and rivers of ale.
The laughter rolled on, like a river so wide,
As critters danced round, no one dared to hide!

Colors of Dusk in the Breaks of Green

At dusk when the colors began to parade,
A parrot wore glasses; it looked rather laid.
The fireflies flashed like a disco ball bright,
While owls dropped beats in the coolness of night.

A raccoon wore ironed clothes, quite a sight,
He juggled ripe berries, oh, what a delight!
The moon had a grin, as it peeked through the trees,
While laughter broke out in the warm evening breeze.

A Patchwork of Nature's Poetry

In the garden, a squirrel runs,
Chasing shadows, having fun.
A daisy laughs, a rose will tease,
As ants hold meetings with great ease.

Pinecones tumble, rolling free,
Bouncing merrily like a glee.
A worm recites its squiggly rhyme,
While flowers dance, it's showtime!

A butterfly sports a polka dot dress,
Winks at a weed, what a mess!
The sunbeams giggle on the grass,
While sprouts join in the joyous class.

So here in nature, all is bright,
With quirky creatures, such delight.
Every corner hides a joke,
In this patchwork, life is woke.

Glistening Tears on Fallen Leaves

Raindrops weep on amber leaves,
Dancing down like nature weaves.
A snail wears his tiny hat,
As puddles form—a custom spat.

The willow whispers, 'What a show!'
As frogs croak tunes—to and fro!
They leap about in slick ballet,
While children splash and laugh away.

A tired beetle sighs with glee,
In mud, a home for it to be.
He dreams of journeys, skies so blue,
Yet gets stuck—oh, what a view!

In every tear that falls today,
There's humor in their wet parade.
Fallen leaves turn into slides,
Where joy and laughter ever bides.

The Heartbeat of the Overgrown

In the thicket, frogs set the beat,
Their ribbits dance beneath my feet.
A hedgehog checks his puffy style,
As nature's chaos makes me smile.

Vines untangle, telling tales,
Of runaway cats and spoofed snails.
The old oak chuckles, wise and stout,
His branches sway, no shadow of doubt.

A raccoon rolls in clumps of grass,
Declaring loudly, 'I'm first in class!'
Beneath the leaves, the fox's sneer,
Confirms that silliness is near.

With every rustle, giggles rise,
Amongst the twigs and fluttering flies.
In this wild world, fun is found,
As laughter sings in every sound.

Stories Entwined in Bristly Embrace

In the thorns, a tale unfolds,
Of mischievous cats and brave little folds.
A bramble's hug is tight today,
As squirrels plot in a cheeky way.

Lizards lounge in a sunlit trace,
Critiquing the flowers with silly grace.
Ants march on, a conga line,
As they search for snacks, oh how divine!

A wise old turtle takes a stand,
Declaring his shell's a mighty brand.
With laughter echoing all around,
Nature's circus is tightly wound.

Each bristle holds a secret laugh,
A wild world writes its funny half.
In every twist and crooked line,
Lie stories endless, pure, divine.

Where Dreams Meet the Dim-lit Brush

In a forest where whispers sway,
Squirrels debate their nuts all day.
A raccoon in slippers, quite the sight,
Dreams of mischief under moonlight.

With shifty eyes and a grin so wide,
Every twig is a place to hide.
Echoes of laughter through the trees,
As frogs in tuxedos hop with ease.

Glimmers Among the Leafy Shadows

A hedgehog wearing a tiny hat,
Said to a snail, 'I'll race you, brat!'
They spun through leaves, both quick and slick,
While butterflies cheered with a little flick.

In the shade, the berries gleam and glow,
But watch out for the cheeky crow!
He'll steal your snack, then wink and fly,
Leaving all critters to wonder why.

Flowing Streams through Knotty Bark

A beaver with dreams of grand design,
Constructed a dam, but oh, how it shined!
His buddies laughed, 'It's quite a feat!'
As squirrels invited him for a treat.

Down the brook, a fish wore a tie,
Said, 'I'm here for the party, oh my, oh my!'
They danced on the waves, a splish and a splash,
Turning the stream into a wild bash.

The Dance of Shadows and Sunbeams

A spider spun silk with flair and pride,
Declared, 'My webs are a joyride!'
As fireflies joined in a dazzling spin,
The forest floor hosted a whimsical din.

The shadows played peek-a-boo with the light,
While rabbits hopped in a comical fight.
They tripped on roots, fell flat on their backs,
Laughter erupted, the best of laughs!

Unearthed Memories of Old Growth

In the woods where whispers play,
Old trees dance in a funny way.
Forgotten secrets, roots entangle,
Laughter hides where shadows wrangle.

A squirrel fights a branch for cheer,
Wearing acorns like a crown, oh dear!
With wobbly steps, he takes his flight,
Over bumpy paths, what a sight!

Mossy carpets, soft and green,
Hide giggles where none have been.
A chatterbox of leaves above,
Telling tales of old forest love.

Nature's glee in every twist,
Who knew limbs could give such a list?
As leaves rustle in playful chat,
The forest floor just loves to spat.

Dappled Light and Hidden Life

Sunbeams tickle through the leaves,
Chasing bugs as if they tease.
A fox in shades of orange gleams,
Stumbles over his daydreams.

Underneath a thicket's fold,
A worm tells jokes that never get old.
With squishy dance and grainy grin,
Everyone joins the silliness within.

Dappled spots where fairies hope,
To find a tiny, laughing rope.
They tie up dreams with strands of cheer,
And swing around without a fear.

What mysteries lie in every nook?
Where critters peek and giggle, look!
Even shadows chuckle low,
At missteps made by the good and slow.

The Serenade of Sylvan Shadows

In twilight's glow, the shadows hum,
Whispers play in the evening's drum.
A raccoon with a mask so sly,
Steals a snack as the owls sigh.

Beneath a branch, a party brews,
With toadstools serving drinks and views.
Crickets sing their evening tune,
While fireflies dance beneath the moon.

Giggles ripple in the night,
As creatures jive in soft twilight.
A hedgehog dons a tiny hat,
And twirls along like fancy chat.

Owl grandpa, with wise old eyes,
Chimes in with jokes that light the skies.
The forest echoes with glee anew,
In a serenade of playful brew.

Memories Encased in Rough Edges

Sticks and stones, they tell a tale,
Of rambunctious fun and trails that fail.
A tumble here, a jump askew,
Each memory wrapped in lumpy glue.

Knots in wood are stories spun,
Of critter games and endless run.
With splintered smiles and jagged turns,
The laughter lingers, the heart still yearns.

Pieces rough, but hearts so free,
In every nook, a jubilee.
Frogs leap high for silly cheers,
While nature catches all their tears.

Misfit joys in wild embrace,
Rough edges carve a smiley face.
Through tangled vines of joke and jest,
The rough and tumble feels the best.

The Language of Rough Textures

Rough and tough, the ground does speak,
Whispering tales to those who seek.
A pebble's chuckle, a twig's guffaw,
Nature's jokes in every flaw.

In every scratch and every groove,
A riddle that no one can prove.
Leaves might snicker, winds might jest,
In the chaos, laughter's the best.

Uneven surfaces bring delight,
A rocky road may cause a fright.
But oh, the smiles that might appear,
When stubs and trips bring us near.

So next time you stop for a stare,
Recall the humor hidden there.
In twists and turns, there's wonders found,
In the textures, giggles abound.

Secrets Hold in Mossy Cracks

In hidden nooks where secrets lie,
Mossy whispers make us sigh.
Aspired dreams in green embrace,
Life's little quirks in quiet space.

Fungi grin with silly hats,
Busy ants in careless chats.
What's that? A beetle's tiny dance,
Nature's stage—give it a chance!

Cracks and crevices, a grand parade,
Where stories of old are softly laid.
Each tiny crevice, a smile to wear,
As silly shadows play everywhere.

What laughs we find in nature's gaps,
Where life's a comic and time just naps.
So peer closely and you might see,
The humor that lives so carefreely.

Fragments of Nature's Lament

Crisp leaves flutter with snorts and snickers,
Twigs bend low like grumpy flickers.
Nature sighs, but laughs instead,
In soft, rustling, leafy bed.

Every spill of seed and shell,
Tells a story, weaving well.
With crackling voice, the branches talk,
Comical tales as they mock the walk.

Fragments scatter, a playful spree,
Lament turned jest, oh can't you see?
Each pebbled path, each crumbled stone,
Holds laughter in nature's tone.

So, listen close to what they share,
For in their growls, joy is rare.
Embrace the funny, the odd, the sweet,
In nature's tale, we find our feet.

Woven Tales of Twisted Twigs

Twisted twigs in jumbles speak,
Winding jokes in whispers weak.
Nature strings a funny tale,
In split bark, we'll never fail.

A squirrel trips, an acorn flies,
Laughter dances in the skies.
With every bend, a jest is spun,
In leafy laughter, we all have fun.

Knotty branches tease the wind,
A conundrum that never thinned.
For every twist, there's humor brewing,
In tangled woods, the joy is stewing.

So raise a cheer for the crooked paths,
Where every misstep fuels the laughs.
With every twist in nature's guise,
We find the funny in all surprise!

Intricate Patterns in the Thicket's Heart

In the thicket, shapes do dance,
Twisting vines take a chance.
A squirrel tries to win his game,
But trips on roots that have no name.

A hedgehog rolls beneath a bush,
While passing by, a rabbit's rush.
With every twist, the shadows shout,
Frogs croak loud, they're hoping out!

A raccoon's hat, askew and neat,
Sneaks through leaves with nimble feet.
Beneath the branches overhead,
A crafty fox dreams of his bread.

Mice make merry, a tiny feast,
While giggling snails come for a feast.
With a wink, the owl will say,
"Join the fun in this wild ballet!"

Flickers in the Underbrush

A firefly glows where shadows creep,
Dancing 'round as others sleep.
A bug's a-drift with wiggly jive,
In tangled weeds, they come alive.

Squirrels squabble, oh what a scene,
Chasing each other, quite obscene.
In pursuit of nuts, they roll and flip,
Turning the ground into a slip.

The porcupine's wearing a spiky crown,
Puffing up like he's never down.
While lowly ants do march and sing,
Under the boughs, they're quite a thing!

With laughter echoing near and far,
The woods become a raucous bazaar.
The underbrush, a lively stage,
Where playful antics never age.

The Call of the Wild and Winding Boughs

Calls from the wild, echoes so bright,
A creature giggles at the moonlight.
Twisted branches, a merry maze,
Guide weary friends through hazy haze.

A playful raccoon juggles pine cones,
While birds tease him with cheerful tones.
The shadows whisper, 'Join the fun!'
As critters gather, one by one.

Fluttering leaves sing a crisp song,
While mischief plays where things go wrong.
Chasing shadows, they tumble and twirl,
Nature's party, give a whirl!

With every rustle, laughter resounds,
The wild's a stage where joy abounds.
So come join the dance, don't be shy,
In the winding boughs, let spirits fly!

Hiding Places in the Chaotic Wild

In chaos deep, a giggle stirs,
Where foliage hums and nature whirs.
A little critter peeks from the den,
Dodging branches, hopping again.

Behind the thorns, a prankster waits,
To pounce on friends, oh what debates!
"Did you see that?" the sparrow squeaks,
While frisky foxes play hide-and-seek.

Acorns tumble, a muffled thud,
As laughter flitters like a light flood.
Caterpillars waddle with graceful flair,
While daisies peek through without a care.

In the wild's embrace, humor flows,
A lively place where mischief glows.
So tiptoe through the leafy scheme,
And join the fun, let's live the dream!

Solitary Figures in the Murmuring Meadow

In the meadow where shadows dance,
A squirrel tells jokes, not a single chance.
Grass tickles toes, laughter's the call,
As daisies roll over, having a ball.

A lone cat prances with twitching ears,
Chasing the wind, despite its fears.
Frogs croak encrypted giggles at night,
While crickets compete in a chirping fight.

A sheep in the corner, a sandwich afoul,
Munching on clovers with a humorous growl.
The sky paints a canvas, patchy and bright,
As we chortle at clouds, like fluffy delight.

So let's trot through this comedy show,
With worms wearing hats, and the stars a-glow.
Embrace the mirth in the meadows' expanse,
Where laughter's the dance and joy takes a chance.

Revelations Beneath the Canopy's Fold

Under leafy whispers, secrets abound,
A raccoon with mischief is joyfully found.
Branches adorned with a squirrel's bright stash,
As owls give a wink with a highly wise splash.

A snicker erupts as branches entwine,
Leaves dressed in puns, quite quirky, benign.
Laughter erupts from an audience shy,
The thrush cracks a joke while perched in the sky.

Frogs in tuxedos make quite the scene,
Crooning to insects, where no one is keen.
The canopy echoes with giggles that twirl,
As nature's confessions make daily life swirl.

Take heed in the laughter, embrace the cheer,
For even the trees have their jokes, never fear.
Beneath all this green, where dance does unfold,
Life's comical hidden, it's worth more than gold.

Shattered Light on the Forest Edge

Sunlight's a jester in the high trees,
Creating a spotlight for the bumbling bees.
Mushrooms are staging their own mushroom play,
While shadows behind them are giggling away.

A wise old turtle speaks riddles and rhymes,
Daring the rabbits to race all the times.
The sunbeams applaud as they bounce off the leaves,
Echoing high with the laughter of thieves.

A fox plays peek-a-boo, no need to chase,
As porcupines join in the joyful embrace.
Dandelions fluff with a tickle and tease,
Spreading petite chuckles with every wild breeze.

In the shimmer and shine where the fun never ends,
Every creature a player, every glance a friend.
In the midst of the trees, we find wisdom in jest,
For nature's a comedy, and laughter's the best.

Forms of Life Beneath the Surface

Under the pond where secrets mix,
Bubbles laugh softly, their playful tricks.
Fish in tuxedos swim to the beat,
While reeds murmur jokes to the ducks on their feet.

Worms host a party beneath all the mud,
While snails slide gracefully, a gooey flood.
The dragonfly flutters with a wink and a spin,
Making the pond throw a giggling grin.

Tadpoles debate what it means to be cool,
As frogs play the drums, they're nobody's fool.
Their croaks add the bass in a watery groove,
A symphony crafted, each creature can move.

So dive in the laughter, let nothing go wrong,
For each splash in the water sings its own song.
In this hidden world where the fun blooms bright,
Life's playful spirit is a comical sight.

Chasing Shadows in the Underbrush

In the thick of night, we scurry around,
A raccoon in pajamas can easily be found.
With limbs like spaghetti, we trip and we laugh,
Dancing with shadows, our own silly gaffe.

We run from the owls, who hoot and who stare,
And dream of adventures in places so rare.
With each lumpy bump of these wild, playful trails,
We'll spin tales of glory with exaggerated tales.

Jumping over stumps like we're flying on dreams,
While chasing our shadows beneath moonlight beams.
The crickets are playing a tune that we know,
As we trip in the dark, on our toes, we will go.

With giggles echoing through leaves and through hay,
We're the rulers of twilight, or so we all say.
So join in the madness, don't leave us alone,
For when night falls upon us, we're never outgrown.

Echoes of the Knotted Trees

The trees are all tangled, how silly they seem,
Their branches are gossiping, waking our dream.
Whispers of woodpeckers tap-tapping in jest,
While squirrels in bow ties are dressed for a fest.

In circles we tumble, like leaves on a breeze,
Playing tag with the shadows, and laughing with ease.
Each step is a pratfall, a chorus of cheer,
As our roots become tangled, we dreadfully fear.

A raccoon spills secrets from under a log,
While a hedgehog joins in, our own little cog.
We'll dance like two whisks in an odd little whirl,
Spinning our stories, oh such a grand swirl!

Echoes of laughter ring deep in the night,
As owls raise their brows, questioning our flight.
Amongst the mischief, we find our delight,
Twisting and tumbling, till dawn's golden light.

Tangles of Time and Twigs

Oh, twigs of all sizes, how goofy you are,
With knots and with tangles, you take it too far.
While rabbits in hats laugh, the fun never quits,
In a wacky old world, where whimsy outwits.

The forest is swirling, just like in a dream,
Where pinecones don top hats and dance by the stream.
And when mischief strikes, we'll surely arise,
With giggles like bubbles that float to the skies.

Backwards we scamper, through bushes and brambles,
In pursuit of a squirrel that out-foxes our gambles.
"Catch me if you can!" he yells from a tree,
As we trip on our shoelaces, wild as can be.

Time twirls like a leaf, in a breeze full of grace,
As we spin and we tumble, enjoying the chase.
For laughter is timeless, and joy it always brings,
In this wacky adventure where all nature sings.

Hidden Trails of the Verdant Wild

In the wild woods we wander, with giggles galore,
Where minnows wear sneakers and dance on the shore.
The underbrush chuckles, with each rustling breeze,
As we trip on the roots and get stuck in the trees.

Marshmallows and mushrooms throw a grand gala,
As we dodge all the critters doing the cha-cha.
Each step brings more laughter, each turn is a jest,
In this realm of the silly, we feel truly blessed.

A trail made of whispers, we leap down the path,
With bushes that tickle and tease with their math.
We're pirates of laughter, on whimsical quests,
While little green fairies host hilarious fests.

So come join the party, oh bring your delight,
For the wild is a jester that twirls in the night.
With hidden trails leading to where giggles unite,
We'll embrace all the madness, till morning's first light.

Wild Aromas on Winding Trails

There once was a scent, quite divine,
A whiff of the cheese left to shine.
It danced through the trees,
Brought squirrels to their knees.

Next came a bloom, oh so bright,
A flower that dared to take flight.
It tickled the nose,
Of a curious prose.

With bees in a conga line swirl,
They buzzed 'round a leaf like a girl.
Each flower a prize,
To the bees' great surprise!

A stroll through the woods, what a treat,
With nature's odd flavors to greet.
Come smell what abounds,
In these frolicking grounds!

Threads Through Thickets of Enchantment

In a patch where the threads intertwine,
Knitters appear, each sipping on wine.
They laugh as they stitch,
At a misdeduced quitch,

With needles a-clatter, they gleam,
While unraveling quite the odd seam.
A mouse on a lark,
Took a bite of their yarn.

The hedgehogs then giggled and played,
As they wove through the thistles so frayed.
They turned into hats,
For the cats' fancy chats!

So tiptoe with joy through the maze,
Unravel the fun in these ways.
For laughter's the thread,
That twirls in your head!

Reflections Among the Weller Wands.

In the glade where the reflections gleam,
Woodies clash for the oddest dream.
They ponder their fate,
While squawking at fate!

A stick with a hat, what a sight,
A pinecone wearing glasses, how bright!
They wiggle and jive,
As the critters arrive.

With jokes that are quirky and light,
Each tale is a burst of delight.
The ponds laugh back,
At their comedic act!

Across every log, a surprise,
Where giggles and chuckles do rise.
For woodland can cheer,
When whimsy is near!

Whispers of the Woodland

In the breeze, there are secrets galore,
Whispers of nonsense, oh, what a score!
The trees tell a tale,
Of a snail on a gale,

Who skipped and who slipped on a shoe,
Made of leaves with a berry or two.
The rabbits just cackled,
As the sunshine unpacked.

Through meadows where giggles unfurl,
Chasing after the cheekiest swirl,
The frogs sing along,
In their silly song.

So wander these paths filled with glee,
Where laughter blooms wild and free.
In delight, we pursue,
Nature's grand comedy!

Journeys Among the Eldritch Foliage

In the woods where shadows play,
I tripped on roots that led astray.
A squirrel laughed and took my hat,
I swear that critter looked quite fat.

A leaping frog said, "Hop along!"
I joined the dance, we sang a song.
But then I fell into a stream,
Who knew that logs could cause such a theme?

With every step, a new surprise,
A dizzy whirl of mischief lies.
I met a fox who told me jokes,
And then he ran off with the folks.

The trees are filled with giggles and glee,
Where every branch welcomes you and me.
A tangled path, oh what a sight,
In this green world, we'll laugh tonight!

Mysteries of the Tangled Grove

Deep in the woods, where whispers creep,
I found a sign that said, "Giggle Deep."
The owls were wise, their jokes were sly,
But every punchline made me cry.

A thicket swept across my shoe,
I dodged and leapt, then fell right through.
The brambles snickered, wove a net,
I'm stuck for sure; what a safe bet!

The gnomes threw a party, oh what a scene,
With tiny hats and loads of green.
They danced on mushrooms, feeling spry,
While I just watched, a baffled sigh.

From tangled twists, laughs always bloom,
Where nature's charm dispels the gloom.
With every snare, there's joy in the fray,
Adventure awaits in a comical way!

The Echoing Heart of the Wild

Amidst the trees, a chortle rang,
As nature's heart began to clang.
A rabbit donned a top hat tight,
As twilight fell and starry night.

With limbs that danced in funny tunes,
We skipped along beneath the moons.
A hedgehog joined in on the beat,
His tiny quills made it quite a feat.

The echoing laughter of the bramble crew,
With every giggle, the trees just grew.
A parrot squawked, "Let's play charades!"
We stumbled through the leafy parades.

All mysteries spill from every leaf,
With laughter sprouting, the world's belief.
In wildest woods, let's make a scene,
As joy and jests make the finest sheen!

Cloaked in Canopy and Mystery

Under the cloak of leafy spree,
I found a raccoon counting to three.
With bandit eyes and a striped tail bright,
He said, "Guess who's stealing snacks tonight!"

I tried to catch him, didn't succeed,
Tripped over roots, a humbled breed.
The crickets chuckled, making a fuss,
While I declared, "I'm not one of us!"

A lantern bug lit the way with cheer,
"Follow me, and you'll see, my dear!"
But tangled limbs only led me astray,
As the forest erupted in a playful fray.

In the teasing light and hidden grooves,
The forest laughs and so do we move.
With smiles shared in every branch,
Nature's funny side is quite the chance!

Tangles of Time Beneath the Canopy

In a forest where squirrels steal,
Time twists like a rubber meal.
Branches gossip, leaves that chat,
Watch out for that slippy mat!

A raccoon played a guessing game,
With a porcupine who had no shame.
They tripped on roots, oh what a sight,
Dancing under the moonlight!

Whispers float like bubbles fair,
While owls twirl without a care.
The clock's hands are all entwined,
In this laughter that's unconfined!

So if you wander here sometime,
Beware of laughter's silly climb.
For in this world of twist and shout,
You'll lose your socks, without a doubt!

Echoes in the Underbrush

In the thicket where shadows play,
Echoes giggle the day away.
A fox in socks tries to impress,
But stumbles in a playful mess!

The bushes chuckle and shake with glee,
As a rabbit spills its cup of tea.
A frog sings out of tune, oh dear,
His croaks and croon are loud and clear!

Crickets join in like a band,
Creating chaos, oh, it's grand!
With rustling leaves as their drumbeat,
Nature's music can't be beat!

If you hear laughter while you stroll,
Don't be alarmed; that's nature's goal.
Join the fun in the leafy wash,
And let out a giggle, in a flash!

Knotted Roots and Gnarled Dreams

Where roots are tangled like old vines,
Dreams dance softly, crossing lines.
A turtle wears a sprinkle hat,
While squirrels tackle acorn sport—how fat!

In this woodland of crazy flights,
Bumblebees wear tiny lights.
A spidery web is a shimmering stage,
Where fireflies steal the show, such rage!

The mushrooms twirl in a silly spree,
While hedgehogs play hide and seek with glee.
Lost in the fun, they giggle loud,
A motley crew, oh, proud and proud!

So tiptoe gently where wonders loom,
For laughter blooms in every room.
When roots and dreams begin to twist,
You'll find yourself in a joyful mist!

Shadows of Twisted Vines

In the shadows where gnomes reside,
Twisted vines spread far and wide.
A raccoon wears a stylish tie,
While birds in hats just laugh and fly!

Laughter bounces from tree to tree,
As mushrooms nod, they just agree.
A snake plays hopscotch, oh what flair,
While owls gossip without a care!

The caterpillars dance on toes,
While the dirt beneath them gently glows.
With each step, giggles intertwine,
In this world of shadows, oh so fine!

So wander with joy where vines embrace,
And find your smile, your happy place.
When shadows twirl and laughter swells,
You'll hear the forest's playful bells!

Dance of the Gnarled Limbs

In a forest where the branches twist,
The trees throw a party, can't resist.
With limbs all tangled, swaying in glee,
Even the roots join in, oh what a spree!

The squirrels are jiving, the owls look on,
A funky beat drops from dusk till dawn.
Moss-covered shoes, hip and ever so sly,
Who knew that trees could dance, oh my!

Leaves spin like tops, round and round,
As acorns drop down, thuds on the ground.
With laughter echoing, all the critters cheer,
In a shindig of shadows, they're full of good cheer!

So if you stroll past the gnarled old trees,
Don't be surprised if you catch the breeze.
Join in their waltz, let loose your own jig,
Life's just a hoot when you dance like a twig!

Serpentines of Ivy and Moss

Ivy's slink like a dancer, smooth and sly,
Wrapping up branches as if to spy.
Moss giggles softly, tickling the bark,
Where sunlight dapples and shadows embark.

The hedgehogs waddle, quite bent out of shape,
While snails in their shells dream of escape.
A chorus of chirps, a raucous delight,
In this leafy maze, there's charm in the bite.

The fungi pop up, with a laugh and a grin,
Mushrooms hold parties where no one can win.
With vine-covered jokes and a spongy old jest,
Who knew that the jungle could be quite the fest?

Join in the fun where the twists run wild,
Nature's a circus, and we're all beguiled.
So giggle with clovers and dance through the dew,
In the winding embrace of the green and the blue!

Sunlight in the Gloomy Glade

In a shadowy nook where the critters reside,
Sunbeams break through, brightening the tide.
Mushrooms all giggle, leaning each way,
Can fungus really boast? Well, they'll have their say!

The bunnies bounce in, with fluff and with fluff,
While the crows shoot jibes, thinking they're tough.
"Your ears are too long," they caw in a tease,
But the bunnies just laugh, saying, "At least we're at ease!"

In this glade of mystery, antics unfold,
With stories of tricksters, both brazen and bold.
A lizard performs with a twist of a tail,
As shadows dance lightly, reciting their tale.

So bathe in the sunlight, let laughter ignite,
In the gloomy old glade where there's always delight.
Catch the whimsy of nature, so odd yet so bright,
For even in darkness, there's joy to incite!

The Language of Leaves and Twine

Once leaves whispered secrets, snug in their beds,
While twine spun tales of what nature spreads.
"Did you hear the pine's awful pun?" they would share,
A raucous old joke carried round with the air.

The ferns curl up, giggling soft in the breeze,
Making jokes 'bout the trees getting lost in the tease.
"Don't branch out too far!" one leaf quips with flair,
"Or you'll end up stuck in a leaf-catcher's snare!"

Vines wrap around, a tangle of lines,
Discussing the weather and playful designs.
With roots in the dirt and fruit overhead,
Nature's own humor keeps all spirits fed.

So lean in and listen, it's quite an affair,
The chatter of greenery fills every layer.
With gales of laughter and joy intertwined,
In the woodland's embrace, we're all redefined!

Glistening Dew on Obscured Paths

Each morning greets with sneaky drops,
That dance on leaves, and never stop.
A slippery slide for my poor feet,
I tumble once, and land in sweet.

The trails are dizzy with glisten and cheer,
But watch for the puddles that may appear.
They hide like a trickster in the grass,
Causing me to stumble and easily pass.

The sun peeks out, a mischievous grin,
My shoes now drenched, it's a new kind of sin.
I laugh through the splashes, with glee in my soul,
For puddles and giggles, they do take their toll.

Soon the paths dry, under the sun's gaze,
And I'll tell the tales of my slippery days.
With chuckles and wriggles, it's all in good fun,
I'll conquer these trails, one splash at a run.

Lanterns of Fireflies in the Brush

Tiny lanterns sparkling bright,
Dancing in the air, a whimsical sight.
With one little hop, I join the parade,
As they flicker and flirt, in evening's cascade.

A glow like confetti in the thick of the night,
I wave to the bug parade in delight.
They dart past my nose, like friends on a spree,
"Hey, come play with us!" they giggle in glee.

But alas! I stumble, and swat at the swarm,
Trying to catch one, oh, isn't it warm?
I trip in the shadows, roll over a stone,
Their laughter echoes, it's like I'm not alone.

Yet through all the chaos I can't keep a frown,
For the fireflies sparkle; they're the stars in my gown.
A dance of pure joy, I won't miss my chance,
Tonight's a wild night, a bug-filled romance.

Muted Colors of the Dappled Sun

In the shade of the trees, where whispers reside,
A canvas of hues, where fantasies hide.
I skip like a pebble on paths overlaid,
With earthy confetti, the joy that I've made.

Muddy brown, and greens that blend,
My socks turn to sketchbooks, I only pretend.
With each little skip, there's a splatter of color,
My shoes now creations, a messy go-stir.

With a giggle I notice a toadstool parade,
They sprinkle the floor, like a cap made of jade.
I stumble and chuckle, for who made the rules?
That nature's a poet, and we're all just fools.

In this muted delight, I twirl with glee,
With paint-like reflections in the canopy tree.
While I slip in the brushes, I'm destined to roam,
For in muddles and giggles, I've found my true home.

Boughs that Bend and Break

Oh, bending branches, what a sight,
Swinging low, like they're ready to fight.
I leap and I dodge, in a playful dance,
But these leafy ninjas, they've got their own plans.

I giggle and wiggle, trying to be sly,
Suddenly a branch gives a creaky sigh.
The rustle of leaves, a mischievous sound,
As I duck and I dodge in my overly round.

I reach for a snack from the generous loot,
But the branch has its thoughts, and it's quite astute.
A thwack on the head, it's a plant-based attack,
With laughter I learn, never look back.

But no matter the tumbles, my heart knows the score,
The boughs may bend, but they never bore.
Each twist and each turn, it's a game that I take,
Among laughing branches, it's all in the shake.

The Hidden Soul of the Thicket

In the woods, a squirrel pranced,
With acorns in his hands, he danced.
A chipmunk joined with a merry squeak,
Their antics left the trees to creak.

A wise old owl perched high with pride,
Questioned where all this laughter hides.
He thought of wisdom, but here's the truth:
Those nuts are just for playful youth!

A dandy deer with spots galore,
Told the tales of a forest lore.
But who needs tales of fearsome fright,
When giggles echo, pure delight?

Down below, where shadows play,
All creatures dance the night away.
In this thicket, jesters roam,
Making the wild their joyful home.

Serenity Within the Wilderness

By the creek, a frog sings loud,
In a chorus, he feels proud.
A turtle nods in gentle ease,
While ants prepare a picnic tease.

A raccoon comes to steal a bite,
But the food trucks off at night!
He trips and slips, what a grand show,
Now frog and turtle laugh in tow.

A rabbit's wearing a fancy hat,
While birds all giggle, imagine that!
In this quiet, silly space,
Nature's laughter fills the place.

So here we find in wild embrace,
A joy that wears a funny face.
In peaceful woods where jokes are spun,
Serenity's just a laugh, they've won!

Vines of Memory and Mirth

Tangled vines twist and twine,
Holding stories, oh so fine.
A monkey swings from branch to branch,
With his silly banana dance.

The rabbit's laughter echoes wide,
As he tries to jump and hide.
Behind the leaves, he thinks he's sly,
But squirrels spot him with a sigh!

The wise old hedgehog joins the brawl,
With quills so sharp, he won't fall.
He shares his wisdom with a grin,
"Just spin and twirl, let fun begin!"

In this jungle, bright and bold,
The vines tell secrets, never old.
Through laughter's embrace, we find the way,
To dance through life in joy each day.

Shadows Play Upon the Ground

As sunbeams stretch and shadows twist,
A cat pounces like he's missed.
With a leap and a funny yowl,
He thinks he's fierce, a mighty prowl.

A hedgehog laughs from a shady nook,
While birds dive down for a silly look.
In this light, who cares about the gloom?
When they can bring the laughter boom!

A raccoon rolls in a pile of leaves,
Decorating with nature's cleaves.
His mud-streaked face, a comical sight,
Makes creatures giggle, oh what a night!

So shadows dance in the playful air,
Chasing joy without a care.
In each corner, fun is found,
As shadows play upon the ground.

Muffled Crunches in Forgotten Paths

In leaves that snap beneath my shoes,
I dance like a squirrel with nothing to lose.
With each wee crunch, a giggle escapes,
Nature laughs back, in odd little shapes.

A stick that pokes as I prance around,
Makes me wonder what treasures I've found.
Each sound a riddle, a joke from the earth,
A comedy sketch of unmeasured worth.

I trip over roots, a sight to behold,
The trees shake their heads, or so I've been told.
With every misstep, a chuckle I share,
The forest is witness—nobody cares!

What's underfoot, a slapstick ballet,
A ticklish romp in a woodland bray.
So come join me, where laughter is free,
In forgotten paths, just you, and the spree!

Caress of Roughened Skin

Oh, the tender touch of nature's embrace,
Leaves scratch my arms, a ticklish race.
With brambles that tug like they mean it in fun,
I laugh and I scratch, under the sun.

A hug from a tree, it's not quite a hug,
More like a poke, friendly snug as a bug.
Roughened skin tells tales of wild romps and plays,
In nature's odd dance, we sing and we sway.

Each branch a therapist, games to unwind,
In pricks and in pinches, the joy I find.
"See how I'm itching? Is this all your fault?"
The leaves just chuckle in an earthy sprawl.

With nature's caress, I ponder and grin,
Life is a riot, where chaos begins.
Embrace all the scrapes, the cuts, and the tears,
For laughter's the cure, as love often dares!

Enigmas of Earthy Layers

Oh, layers of dirt, you clever disguise,
Playing hide and seek with unsuspecting eyes.
What's buried beneath? A mystery's call,
With worms writing riddles, let's solve them all!

In every small mound, secrets reside,
A toe-stubbing bump, oh how can I slide?
I trip over thoughts as I rummage around,
Where giggles and wiggles in compost abound.

Roots intertwined, like old friends in cheer,
Sharing tales of the season, both far and near.
The soil does chuckle with every small quake,
In the enigma's laughter, the whole world wakes.

So let's dig and bluff where the wild things grow,
In the game of the earth, we'll laugh and we'll glow.
These riddles of nature bring smiles and delight,
In a journey of whimsy, we revel in light!

Beneath the Thicket's Veil

Underneath the thicket, I shuffle along,
With branches that whisper a mischievous song.
Each tangled vine has a punchline to share,
Nature's own stand-up, beyond all compare.

I duck and I weave through the leafy abode,
And twigs scratch my back like I'm riding a toad.
A soft, squishy spot—what's hidden in there?
Just a squirrel's dinner! Well, think I'll not share.

Laughter erupts from the roots of the ground,
As I tumble and stumble—oh, what have I found?
A patch of soft moss, a throne made for me,
I crown myself king of this jester's decree.

So come take a gander, step under and see,
The thicket's hilarity, earthy and free.
In shadows and giggles, we frolic and play,
For life in the wild is a jest every day!

Twilight's Embrace in the Thorns

As I stumbled through the tangled vines,
A poky prince, I seized the lines.
With leaves that giggle, branches tease,
I danced the waltz of prickled trees.

Moonlight casts a shadowed guise,
Where laughter hides in nature's eyes.
Each twist and turn, a funny fate,
In this thicket, I can't be late.

A squirrel chuckles at my plight,
While I negotiate with bark in sight.
I shout, "You tree, I need a hug!"
But only find a sticky bug.

Promotion signs for scraggly twigs,
Announcing entrances for cheeky digs.
In the chaos, joy finds its way,
In twilight's grip, I'm here to play.

Rift of Roots and Revelations

Underneath the leafy spread,
A riddle rests in mossy bed.
Whispers mingle with the breeze,
Secrets buzz like busy bees.

Roots tangle like my morning hair,
I wiggle free with style so rare.
Must've crossed paths with a clumsy vine,
Doing the twist? Oh, how divine!

Every step, a little trip,
A nature dance, a silly slip.
A rabbit watches, laughing loud,
While I bow to the thicket crowd.

Through leafy gaps, the sunlight beams,
I brush with humor, tripping dreams.
Revelations peek from hidden trails,
In this wild world, my laughter sails.

The Poetry of Prickly Passages

In a forest of tangled aspirations,
Words grow thick in wild formations.
A poke, a jab, a twist of fate,
Embracing each thorn, I celebrate!

With rhymes that scratch and tickle too,
I write my verse in golden dew.
The leaves applaud my witty schemes,
As sunlight dances on my dreams.

From prickly paths, wisdom flows,
A cactus wears a velvet nose.
I laugh with joy at nature's tease,
Finding humor in the floppy breeze.

And when I trip on roots galore,
I stand back up, always wanting more.
In poetry's dance with brambles tight,
I playfully ponder into the night.

Ascent into the Wildwood Whispers

Climbing up the branches high,
Avoiding splinters with a sigh.
Nature giggles, I can hear,
As every tree draws very near.

With a hat made out of leafy tales,
I soar like dreams on gentle gales.
The vines conspire, pulling tight,
Revealing mysteries in their might.

If I trip on this rooftop throne,
I'll tumble fast, yet not alone.
For every crack and crunch beneath,
Is laughter hiding in the wreath.

Wildwood whispers play their tricks,
As I dodge the pokes and pricks.
In this game of hilarity,
I find joy in nature's parody.

Tales from the Tangled Wilderness

In the woods where the raccoons dance,
Squirrels plot their nutty romance.
Trees wear hats made of old shoes,
And critters gossip like afternoon news.

A badger with a beard so grand,
Brags of treasures lost in the sand.
While owls play poker under the stars,
And frogs sing opera from their cars.

Mice on scooters zoom and glide,
Chasing dreams with nothing to hide.
While snails hold a slow-motion race,
And turtles grin with a steady pace.

In this world of silly delight,
Every shadow bursts with light.
When nature laughs, we all should too,
For the wilderness loves a funny view.

Photography of Nature's Decay

The flowers pose in their faded gowns,
Old leaves wear crowns made of frowns.
Mossy stones grumble, 'We've seen it all,'
While termites tap dance at twilight's call.

An aging tree winks with a creak,
Claiming wisdom like an ancient Greek.
With fungi that sprout into artful swirls,
Nature snaps pics of its own twists and twirls.

Beetles flaunt their shiny attire,
As bugs boast a friendship that won't expire.
Roots tangle like gossiping friends,
Sharing secrets that never end.

With every crack and every fissure,
A snapshot held in nature's picture.
Though decay may seem sad and gray,
Even the withered can find a way.

Harmonies of Wild Growth

In a garden of weeds, the chaos sways,
Petunias plot their escape from the rays.
A sunflower winks, 'I'm here to stay,'
While daisies gossip in a bright bouquet.

The carrots hold a concert at dawn,
As radishes shake, 'Don't be a prawn!'
Insects chirp like a kooky band,
With tunes so catchy, they're in high demand.

Vines twist around in a goofy trance,
While clovers sway, inviting romance.
With every leaf, a melody plays,
In this wild symphony, nature betrays.

So join the fun, with every sprout,
For life's a song filled with giggles and shouts.
Where soil's the stage and growth's the show,
Laugh with the plants, let the humor flow.

In the Grip of Nature's Whisper

Oh, the trees, they whisper sweet little lies,
Saying squirrels wear the best of ties.
With branches that stretch like they're having fun,
Tickling the clouds till the day is done.

The wind gives secrets to flowers in bloom,
As bees buzz in circles, creating a room.
While critters share tales of nighttime frights,
Dancing in shadows under pale moonlights.

Rolling stones giggle, they can't be still,
Each mossy patch holds a hidden thrill.
With every rustle, a chuckle doth rise,
As nature's humor is a grand surprise.

So listen close to the earth's soft cheer,
For laughter's hidden in every sphere.
In the grip of nature, all is playful,
Life twirls and tumbles, always grateful.

Forests Guarding Forgotten Tales

In a wood where whispers weave,
The trees giggle, don't believe!
Acorns rolling, play their role,
Squirrels plotting, that's their goal.

Mushrooms dancing, hats so tall,
Frogs in tuxedos, having a ball!
The sun peeks in, a gentle tease,
While shadows chuckle with a breeze.

Old roots grumble, "Who's that there?"
A rabbit twitching—what a scare!
Owls hoot jokes, wisdom so sly,
As raccoons giggle, oh my, oh my!

Tales of the forest, odd and grand,
Mistaken identities at hand.
A hedgehog caught in a dance-off spree,
In this whimsical old greenery!

Pathways of Echoing Crickets

Along the trails, crickets sing,
With chirps that dance and fun they bring.
Frogs croak back, their voices bold,
While fireflies twinkle, tales unfold.

A toad jumps high, a startled leap,
Chasing dreams while crickets peep.
Night's a stage for bugs to play,
In the laughter of the milky way.

Paths of chatter, laughter loud,
Insects juggling, they are proud!
The moonbeam shines, a spotlight bright,
As they perform, under starlight.

Echoing giggles fill the air,
Every hopping friend laid bare.
With muddy feet and joyful glee,
In this concert, wild and free!

The Enchantment of Clinging Ferns

In the nook of nature's twist,
Ferns cling tight, you can't resist.
With their fronds, a leafy tease,
Filtering sun, oh what a breeze!

Dew drops hang like little gems,
Winking at the racing hems.
A snail scurries, oh so slow,
Carrying leaves, his own tableau.

Chipper chipmunks scurry 'round,
Finding treasures in the ground.
Whispers of laughter, flutters near,
As ferns giggle, what a cheer!

Beneath the fronds, a shadowed nest,
Where critters huddle, feeling blessed.
Every twist and turn, a delight,
Magic blooms, hidden from sight!

Heartbeats Beneath the Canopy

Underneath the leafy dome,
Creatures gather, feeling home.
A soft thump thump, what's that sound?
A raccoon dreaming, snuggly bound.

Beneath the moss, a secret beat,
Dances of ants, busy on their feet.
A tapestry of tiny tunes,
While wise old owls chart the moons.

Faint giggles float through the air,
From creatures hidden here and there.
In shadows deep, mischief brews,
As laughter spills in earthy hues.

In whispers soft, the forest hums,
A harmony where laughter comes.
Heartbeats pulse with glee tonight,
Underneath the stars so bright!

The Veiled Secrets of Greenfold

In the woods where shadows prance,
Squirrels plot a nutty dance.
Trees wear hats of mossy style,
While owls hoot and wink awhile.

Mice conduct a tiny band,
Playing tunes of peanut sand.
Worms and grubs all sing along,
To the forest's silly song.

In a nook, a rabbit spies,
Frogs in waistcoats, oh my, oh my!
while hedgehogs argue over snacks,
And hedges hum their witty facts.

Underneath the bustling leaves,
Nonsense lives while laughter weaves.
Every crunch a secret sly,
In the woods, we laugh and cry.

Fractured Dreams in the Understory

Once a mushroom wore a tie,
But lost it to a passing fly.
Snails compete in slow-mo races,
While dandelions puff their faces.

Rabbits in a hat parade,
Dancing on a whisker's blade.
Jellybeans fall from tall trees,
Sticky sweets that drift on breeze.

Beetles take their nightly stroll,
Strumming crickets, that's their goal.
A turtle in a tutu spins,
While laughter echoes, spins, and grins.

A butterfly with sneaky wings,
Whispers jokes and funny things.
Fractured dreams of woodland cheer,
Dance together, year by year.

Stories Woven by Whispering Vines

A vine once claimed it knew the tales,
Of fish who sailed on mushroom gales.
With leaves as pages, words like breeze,
Whispering secrets beneath the trees.

A toad recites with flair and ease,
Of squirrels holding fancy teas.
Where acorns fall like rain from skies,
And twirling leaves wear silly sighs.

The wind comes by—a storyteller,
Gossiping like a nosy feller.
It tells of cat's dreams in the sun,
And ducks that race just for the fun.

The tales of nature intertwine,
With giggles rolled like summer vine.
In every rustle, every cheer,
Lives a tale to share, my dear.

Labyrinth of the Lush and Lonesome

In a tangle where the wild things cluck,
Dances sprout like gentle luck.
Fireflies play a game of tag,
While twigs unleash their silly brag.

Bumbles bounce from flower to tree,
Gossiping hums so merrily.
Each leaf a note in pranked up tunes,
Where night croons underneath the moons.

A hedgehog maps the winding way,
With quills like needles, come what may.
Hare and fox, in mischief's snare,
Race in circles, no one's aware.

Whispers rise where blooms collide,
In the thicket, laughter's tide.
A labyrinth where joy does roam,
In nature's arms, we find our home.

www.ingramcontent.com/pod-product-compliance
Lightning Source LLC
Chambersburg PA
CBHW071831160426
43209CB00003B/273